MW00390415

Printed in the United States of America.

First Printing, October 2019.
CreateSpace, LLC/Amazon.com

ISBN-13: 978-1695831636

Library of Congress Control Number: 2019915197

Imprint: Independently published

www.TheFinkleyExperience.com

ABOUT THE AUTHOR AND CONSULTING FIRM

The Finkley Experience: *An Educational Consulting Firm* was founded in 2018 by Michael D. Finkley. The Finkley Experience is an educational consulting that specializes in **FIRST GENERATION EDUCATION**. We focus on college readiness for low-income, first generation students. We provide the resources needed for **students** to be successful within the college admissions process while in high school, we train **school administrators** and the state of first generation students and how to educate and prepare their first generation high school population on the college process, and finally, we partner with **colleges/universities** in preparing their first generation college population for an easy transition from high school to college. We focus on college applications, scholarships/financial aid, standardized testing, essay writing, and other documents needed to complete this process.

Finkley holds a Bachelor of Arts in English, Master of Education (k-12), Master of Science in Higher Education Administration, and is a Certified Global Career Development Facilitator. He has assisted students in gaining admission into the following institutions: Allen University, Campbell University, Clemson University, Duke University, Francis Marion University, University of South Carolina, Winthrop University, and the list continues; and has also assisted students in receiving partial/full ride scholarships.

For more information about The Finkley Experience: *An Educational Consulting Firm*, please visit our website @ www.TheFinkleyExperience.com or to **BOOK Finkley**, please email us @ michael@thefinkleyexperience.com.

Dedication

This college readiness guide is dedicated to my mama, Carol Finkley-Nixon, who told me to aim for a career instead of a job. To my step-dad, Isaac Nixon, who did not allow my mama to pick me up when I wanted to drop out of college. To my father, Jerry Owens, who taught me what not to do as a black male in the society. To my sisters, Karibean Finkley and Rakeya Elleby, and brother, Marcus Jackson, who always encouraged me to continue with my dreams and educational goals with a competitive, friendly spirit. And finally, to my niece, Sanaa, and nephews, Jayvion and Jeddiah who continue to push me in hopes for them to have a better educational future.

I love you all!

Your son, brother, and uncle,

Mannie

What's in this Guide?

Introduction

I grow up in a single-parent household where my mama was a strong advocate for education. She would always check the homework of my sisters and I, chaperone field trips, and stayed in constant contact with teachers. Mama always encouraged us to aim for a career instead of a job. For me, this was done by continuing within the arena of education beyond high school. When it was time to apply for college, I was completely lost within the process; so was my mama. All my mama could do at the time was provide me with her information and a ride to my school.

As a first-generation student (a student whose parents/guardians did not complete a two-year and/or four-year college degree), the college process was very tough! I had a high school counselor who did not take the time to explain the necessities needed, so I had to teach myself. And it took too long! I am grateful I had a university family who assisted me through the process, especially the Free Application for Federal Student Aid (FAFSA). But I still missed out on so many other educational opportunities and scholarships.

As life continued, I was employed as a college admission counselor, high school college and career counselor, teacher, career services coordinator, adjunct instructor, and a director of student services. I have gained a lot of information, knowledge, and experience in preparing students for college. I do hope and pray this guide will assist you during your educational journey!

The Finkley Experience Section ONE: *What is College F.I.T.?*
Picture it! You have just finished shopping at the mall, and you purchased that favorite piece of clothing or footwear you have been saving for months. You run home to try it on again! You burst open the door to your room, close the door, and rip open your shopping bag. You slowly place one foot in at a time or carefully place the piece of clothing onto your body. You look in the mirror and say to yourself, "What a perfect College F.I.T.!" This is the same type of feeling and excitement you should have in choosing your college. Whether it is a two-year or four-year school, choosing carefully is the key! Start thinking about the following questions: What do I like to do? How can I turn my passion into my career? What gives me fuel and drive for my passion? Ultimately, what do I want my major/program of study to be?

Why didn't anyone tell me about College F.I.T. when I was thinking about college!?!? I really did not know anything about this concept until I started working professionally. Finding your College F.I.T. is the first step in the process of constructing your plan for college; this is the foundation. Without this foundation, your plan will fall apart. Many people, when thinking about this concept, define it in different ways. This is how I define it: **Future Individual Timeline**. Self-explanatory; right? Well, let's discuss! You, as a future college student, must determine what tasks must be completed at your future alma mater (college/university) for you to be successful as an individual. Does this institution line up with your timeline? This is the time for you to conduct research for yourself of colleges that peak your interest. So, when thinking about your future institution, think about the following questions:

What is the cost of attendance?
(Tuition, Room & Board, Additional Fees)

Can I afford to attend this institution for the
next 2-4 years?

What types of merit-based aid or endowed scholarships
are offered for first-year students?

What other scholarships are offered for current student
at this institution?

Does your institution offer work-study or have a student
employment program?

What is the percentage of students who depend on
financial aid to attend this institution?

Does this institution assist within completing the Free
Application for Federal Student Aid (FAFSA)?

What is the average amount of loans students that
graduate from this institution leave with?

Does this institution have my major/program of study?

Are professors/instructors in my intended major/program of study still in the field?

Are internships/travel aboard opportunities available at this institution?

What is the teacher to student ratio?

Does this institution have the sports program I desire to play? What sports division is this institution?

What is this institution's acceptance rate? (How many students get accepted to this institution?)

What is the retention rate? (How many students stay at this institution after freshman year?)

What is the graduation rate? (How many students graduate on time?)

What is the employment placement rate? (Does the institution assist in finding employment?)

Do I feel at home here? (Self-Reflect on this question)

What is the social life aspect at this institution?
(Clubs, organizations, etc.)

Is your institution diverse?
(Ethnic, Gender, Social-Economic, etc.)

If this institution does not have my social activity, can I start my own?

Does the Student Government Association really have a voice on campus?

If I have a learning disability, will I be accommodated properly?

What type of safety protection does this institution offer?

These are important questions students should ask when shopping around for their College F.I.T. I want to warn you, the College F.I.T. process will have you in your feelings, but it is so worth it at the end! *Therefore, I recommend that a student begin this process freshman year of high school.* Why? That's a GREAT question!

You always want to give yourself time to research, ask questions, and be totally sure about your decision. Attending college to receive a degree, diploma, or certification is something one should not take lightly. College is one of the most expensive investments a person will make in life. Planning this process properly will decrease your chances from transferring from institution to institution and changing your major countless times. As a result, you will owe less money and may even find yourself graduating early from college!

As you start this process your freshman year of high school, create a college list and as you learn more about your institution, keep everything together in one place. It is okay to request information from these institutions including swag (shirts, pennants, hats, etc.). Remember, freshman year of high school is the year of College F.I.T. Research! Research! Research! **I do not recommend touring college campuses during this time.**

The Finkley Experience Section TWO:
Where is the Support?

"When one is helped, many are helped!" I created this quote to capture the importance of helping one another. The purpose is to pay this gesture forward in helping someone else in life; we call it support. I have heard countless times, "Mr. Finkley, I am in my feelings about the college process; this is too hard!" Well, let's find a solution.

Support can come in so many forms including: parents/guardians, school officials, college officials, etc. But let's discuss the support of your TRUE friends. Hi! I get it! You are in high school and I tell you, peer pressure is a struggle. But you must keep the bigger picture in mind; if they are truly your friends, you will lift each other up in your decisions for the future; you all will be on such a positive charge that you will feed off one another easily. Always remember, when one WINS, you all WIN! Let my life be an example for you. My best friend of eighteen years has been that friend who has been through the ringer with me. We have had countless conversations about our futures, hopes, and dreams of leaving the life of poverty to getting our dream jobs and traveling the world. These thoughts stemming from graduating from high school and attending college. With so many obstacles against us, we were determined to make college our golden ticket!

My best friend was one of my many support systems during my college application process. Think about it! Who is a part of your support system? Many do not have the support of family and friends, but you can find support within your high school. While in high school, think about the following suggestions:

✓ If your high school offers the following programs, JOIN ONE: TRiO Programs, GEAR UP, Jobs for America's Graduates (J.A.G), or any other organization with a focus on college/career readiness

✓ Join a national honors society

✓ Student Council

✓ Dual Enrollment/Early College Programs

✓ Join an athletic/academic team

✓ Attend workshops and class meetings conducted by school counselors/college coaches

✓ Get involved within your school and home communities

Make a list of the people in your support circle. Beside each person, describe how they provide support to you during the college admissions process.

The Finkley Experience Section THREE:
College Application Stage

At this stage in the process, you should be very proud of yourself! For the past three years, you have completed all your research of colleges/universities that have peaked your interest. You have even narrowed down your list to your TOP 10 colleges/universities. This process was done by visiting campuses, contacting admission counselors, and chatting with your friends and family members who may have attended these institutions. You are on it! Great job! Now, you are in your first semester as a high school senior. The hard part is behind you. Currently, you are now able to apply to your TOP 10. Depending on your preferred method, there are ample ways to apply to institutions of your choosing. This can be down via the internet or via a paper application.

As you begin completing applications for colleges, you will need important information to complete this task.

This information includes: **Full Legal Name** (This includes your legal first, middle, and last names; students have similar names; this is why this is important to make sure you are you!), **Address** (This is where you live), **Mailing Address** (This is where you receive your mail; this could include post office boxes), **Email Address** (Make sure this address is professional in nature; a standard email will include your first and last name; ex: joedoe@gmail.com), **Citizenship Questions** (These questions are to confirm your citizenship; if you are a U.S. Citizen or not; these types of questions can affect your financial aid when applying to college; answer honestly!), **Social Security Number** (this task can be optional depending on the institution for being admitted; but it is always great to know this number!) **House/Cell Phone Numbers**, **YOUR Birthday**, and **YOUR Parent/Guardian Information** (This information can include a range of information including their names and dependents (if they have other children) to information about their employment/residency). In having this information, you are off to a great start in completing your college applications. Additional sections to look for during the application process include: **Educational Information** (Information about your high school, professional school counselor information, grade point average) and **College Information** (Desired major/program of study, interest in clubs/organizations, goals after graduation OR if you have attended college before. Remember, as a transfer student, information from previous colleges/universities will be needed. Dual enrollment/early college usually do not fit this category, but check with your institution for more information), **Financial Information** (YOUR income from the previous year; parents/guardian income information).

<u>FUN FACT # 1</u>: *Residency information is important to certain institutions especially for technical and community colleges. If wanting to attend a technical or community college, many of these institutions service certain areas or counties; meaning if you do not reside in these areas or counties, you may have to pay an "out of county" fee. Contact the institution's Office of Financial Aid or Office of Admissions for more information.*

Now it is time to write about yourself via an essay. What?? Do not be afraid; this is the time to express to the admissions committee/counselor why you would be the perfect **College F.I.T**. for their institution. This is your time to shine! Some institutions will provide you with a prompt to write upon and some institutions will give you a creative space to write about whatever your heart so desires to discuss. Check out *The Finkley Experience Workbook* for sample essay topics to look out for during the college application process. As you are finishing up your writing process, here are some helpful tips in completing this process:

- ✓ Having your essay edited (checking for grammar, spelling, etc.) by an English teacher
- ✓ Having your essay revised (to rearrange, to alter) by 3-4 people you trust
- ✓ Stay on topic when writing
- ✓ Pay attention to the minimum and maximum word-count requirement
- ✓ If completing an online application (i.e. The Common Application, The Black College Application), some online systems may not allow you to copy and paste your essay; make sure you complete your essay in a Google Document or a Word Format and email to your admission counselor
- ✓ BE YOURSELF!

After submitting your essay, you will need a few more pieces of information. Three important documents needed are: unofficial transcript, ACT/SAT scores, and letters of recommendation.

Unofficial Transcripts

Many students may request their professional school counselor to send their official transcripts to the institutions they are applying to for the fall semester. Let's change this language! Next time you walk into your Student Services Center, request your unofficial transcript. **Transcripts are not official until you graduate from your high school.** Colleges/universities have the power to accept you based on your unofficial transcript. It is okay if you have not completed your senior year yet; institutions of higher learning understand this and have procedures in place to prepare them for your final transcript/grades.

<u>**FUN FACT #2**</u>: *If applying for early action or early decision, you are only submitting grades ranging from freshman year to junior year of high school. After your acceptance, you do have the right to re-submit your 1st and/or 2nd quarter senior grades for review. This could increase your merit-based aid and/or need-based aid.*

Contact the institution's Office of Admissions or Office of Financial Aid for more information about their policies and procedures.

ACT/SAT Scores

College/universities may request your ACT/SAT scores. What is this? I am glad you asked! The American College Test (ACT) and the Scholastic Aptitude Test (SAT) are standardized test used in the college admission process to assist in determining acceptance into a(n) college/university. The ACT consists of four tests including: English, Mathematics, Reading, Science Reasoning, and an optional Writing Assessment. The SAT has four sections including: Reading, Writing and Language, Mathematics (no calculator), and Mathematics (calculator allowed), an optional Writing Assessment. During your freshman year of high school, you may want to begin thinking about taking the Pre-SAT. ***I would highly recommend you discussing this opportunity with*** *your parent/guardian and your professional school counselor.* Also, in some states, students can take the ACT/SAT (your choosing) during their third year of high school. Students can submit these scores during the college admission process of their senior year; this does not include Pre-SAT scores. *Again, I would HIGHLY recommend you discussing this opportunity with your parent/guardian and your professional school counselor.* **TAKE ADVANTAGE OF THESE OPPORTUNITIES!**

As you are researching institutions that meets your **College F.I.T**., you may come across institutions where they are listed as **TEST OPTIONAL**. This means these institutions **DO NOT** require students to submit ACT/SAT scores during the college application process. Many institutions are leaning more to this policy while other institutions are against it. Again, do your research and contact the Office of Admissions at your desired institution(s) for more information.

FUN FACT #3: *Visit the ACT (<u>www.act.org</u>) and SAT (<u>www.collegeboard.org</u>) websites for updated information of dates, times, and location of testing near you.*

Letter of Recommendation

What is a letter of recommendation? Well, think about it like this! Think about the times you were in grade school and you were sick. You would go to the doctor and he/she would give you an excuse saying you were to stay out of school for a certain amount of days and when you return, you must give this excuse to your teacher. Same concept!

You are asking people you know to write letters to your desired institutions while discussing your personality, achievements, and goals. Therefore, you must choose wisely who you allow to write your letter of recommendation. Colleges/universities may state particular people who they would like to see letters from including **professional school counselors, teachers, administrators, community leaders, employers, clergy, etc.** If your desired institutions does not specify, you have the freedom to choose; make sure you choose at least three people you trust and have known you at least two years. During this phase, do not solicit letters from parents/guardians, personal friends, or other relatives. Also, check out *The Finkley Experience Workbook* for an example of a letter of recommendation.

Institutions are included in one of three admission policies; remember these categories and their definitions:

<u>Early Action:</u> acceptance received is nonbinding; students will receive an early response to their application but do not have to commit

<u>Early Decision:</u> acceptance received is binding; students who are accepted must attend the institution

<u>Rolling Admissions:</u> this is an option for students who not wish to choose early action or early decision; this policy offers a large application window for students; colleges/universities respond as the applications come in instead of waiting until after a deadline

The Finkley Experience Section FOUR:
So, What's Financial Aid?

When I was going through the college admission process, paying for college did not cross my mind. I know it does not make sense, but follow me! I thought magically it would pay for itself. Even though I was completing the financial aid process, I still did not know what I was doing and what this process acutally meant to me and my education. But, this is why I say, "Thank God for time!" Time truly reveals all.

Federal Student Aid Identification (FSA ID)

There are major steps in completing your financial aid. In starting this process, students and parents/guardians must receive a Federal Student Aid Identification (FSA ID). The FSA ID is a username and password that is needed to assist in signing your online financial aid application. In this process, be prepared to have the following information on hand: **Creating a username**

and password for your account (Password cannot include any parts of your name, birthday, or social security number; be creative!) **FULL LEGAL Name, Mailing Address, Phone Number (Home or Cell), Social Security Number, Birthday, and Email Address; also, you must provide answers to three challenge questions and create and provide answers to two challenge questions.** The website for the FSA ID: **https://fsaid.ed.gov/npas/index.htm.** Refer to ***The Finkley Experience Workbook*** for the FSA ID Worksheet.

FUN FACT #4:

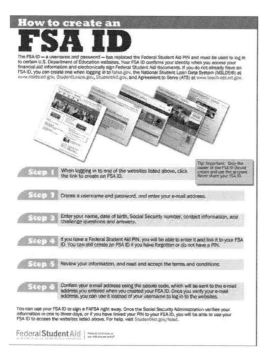

Additional Info about
YOUR FSA ID

- This is your electric signature for the FAFSA (financial aid)
- Both student and parent/ legal guardian need a FSA ID
- This process MUST be done FIRST!

***Once you have submitted your information for your FSA ID, it will take the federal government 1-3 days to verify your information. Once this process is completed, you will receive an email stating your outcome.**

Free Application for Federal Student Aid (FAFSA)

Okay, so you have now completed the FSA ID process!
You have completed 50% of the process. I have seen
many times, students have stopped at this process
thinking they have completed the finanical aid process;
not so! The next step is the Free Application for Federal
Student Aid (FAFSA). The FAFSA is a free, online

application where, based off your income and your parent/legal guardian's income, funds are generated to provide monies to you in paying for college. When you encounter a wesbite asking you for payment to complete the FAFSA, this is the incorrect site; DO NOT input your personal information and exit from the site. Within this financial aid process, you will view methods of receiving money from the federal and state levels; this including: **GRANTS, SCHOLARSHIPS, and LOANS**. We will review these methods later in this section.

To complete the Free Application for Federal Student Aid (FAFSA), you will need:

- ✓ Your Social Security Number
- ✓ Your Alien Registration Number (if you are not a U.S. citizen)
- ✓ Your federal income tax returns, W-2s, and other records of money earned. (**Note:** You may be able to transfer your federal tax return information into your

FAFSA from the IRS using the Data Retrieval Tool.)
- ✓ Bank statements and records of investments (if applicable)
- ✓ Records of untaxed income (if applicable)
- ✓ An FSA ID to sign electronically.

FUN FACT #5:

**October 1st (every year)
The new Free Application for Federal Student Aid (FAFSA) will be available for completion at**
https://studentaid.ed.gov/sa/fafsa

The FAFSA website recently made some changes; with these changes, you will need your FSA ID to log in to begin working on your application. Therefore, it is very important you complete the FSA ID process FIRST! This is the screen you will see when logging into the site:

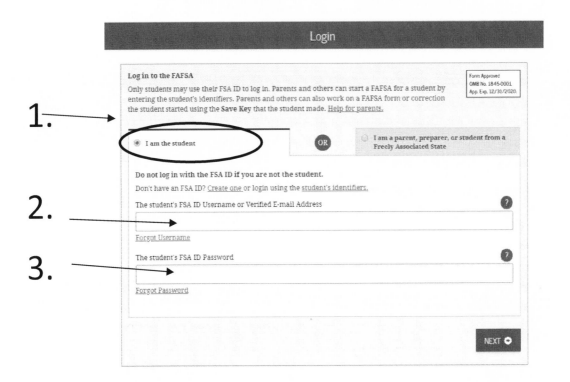

Login-In Page

1. Select the "**I am the student**" tab. The other tab is the parents, preparers (someone you pay to complete your FAFSA), and students from a Freely Associated State (Citizens of the Marshall Islands,

Federated States of Micronesia, and Palau. If you do not have a Social Security Number (SSN) and are not a citizen of the Federated States of Micronesia, the Republic of the Marshall Islands, or Palau, otherwise known as the "Freely Associated States," you cannot complete a FAFSA).

2. Enter your FSA ID Username or Verified Email Address (this is the email address you used when you created your FSA ID profile)

3. Enter your FSA ID Password (Refer back to your FSA ID worksheet provided in *The Finkley Experience Workbook*)

Disclaimer

Please read this disclaimer by the federal government. If you agree with these terms, you will click the **ACCEPT** button, if not, you will click the **DECLINE** button.

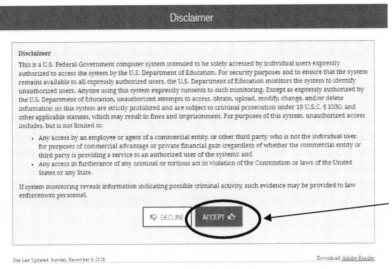

<u>My FAFSA</u>

In this section, it will introduce the new FAFSA academic year at the top; for example: ***My FAFSA- 2019-2020.*** You will then choose which academic year you are completing your application for; you will have two options; the previous year or the current year. *(**If applying to an university/college in the fall semester (August/September), you will complete the FAFSA for the current year; if applying in the spring semester*

(January), you will complete the FAFSA for the previous year.)

Afterwards, you will have two options to start the application process; this is **FAFSA RENEWAL** or **START NEW FAFSA.** The RENEWAL FAFSA option is accessible to you if you filed the FAFSA during the previous award year; it uses demographic data from the previous year's FAFSA to pre-fill this year's FAFSA. If you would just like a fresh start or did not complete a FAFSA the previous year, you will use the START NEW FAFSA option.

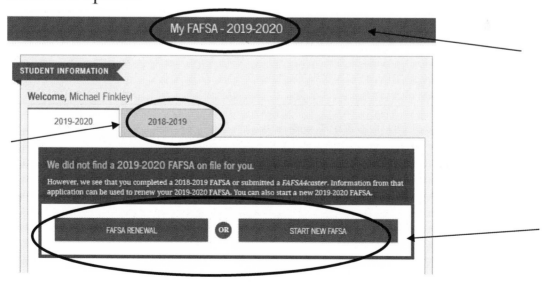

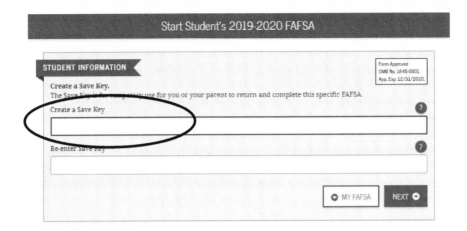

<u>Save Key</u>

For this section, you will create a save key. This is for YOUR protection! Your save key must be between 4-8 characters long. Your save can include numbers, letters (uppercase and lowercase). Make sure you record this save key in a safe place because you will need this information again.

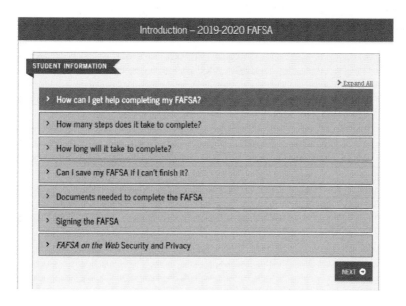

Introduction

In the introductory section, you are able to "preview" each section of the FAFSA. Once you have read each section, click the NEXT button to start your financial aid application.

Student Demographics (Part I)

YAY! You are beginning your finanical aid application for college! This is exciting! If this is your first time completing this process, please have your parent/guardian, professional school counselor, a financial aid counselor, or someone familiar with this process to assist you. You want to make sure all the information you enter is accurate. In this section, you will be inputing: **LAST NAME, FIRST NAME, MIDDLE INTIAL, SOCIAL SECURITY NUMBER**, and **DATE OF BIRTH**. Things to remember: **1)** You are a <u>PROPER NOUN</u> (*a name used for an individual* *person, place, or organization, spelled with initial capital letters*); all proper nouns are capitalized; please, capitalized your last name, first name, and middle intial.

2) Please input your correct social secruity number; please do not guess your number. If you do not know this information, please ask your parent/guardian or professional school counselor.

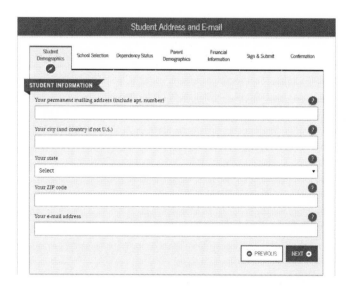

Student Demographics (Part II)

You will need to provide the following information about yourself: **PERMANENT MAILING ADDRESS** (this is the address where you get your mail; this could be different from your physical address; do not include a post office box), **CITY, STATE, ZIP CODE, and E-MAIL ADDRESS** (make sure your e-mail is appropriate).

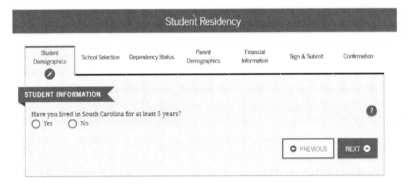

Student Demographics (Part III)

In this section, you will be asked if you have lived in your state for at least 5 years. If you click YES, you are free to continue to the next section. If you click NO, you will be prompted to answer additional questions to where you have resided. Once you have completed that process then press the NEXT button.

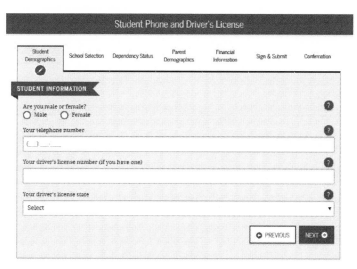

Student Demographics (Part IV)

In this section, you will be asked the following: your legal **GENDER** (male or female), **TELEPHONE NUMBER** (this can include your home phone number or cellular phone number), **DRIVER'S LICENSE NUMBER** (if you do not have a driver's license, you do not have to input any information), and **DRIVER'S LICENSE STATE** (if you do not have a driver's license, you do not have to input any information).

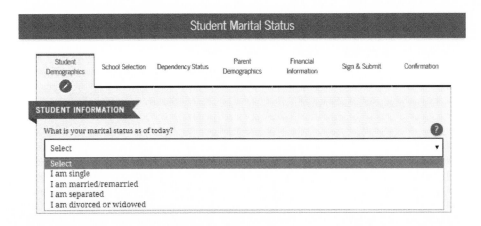

<u>Student Demographics (Part V)</u>

In this section, you (the student) will be asked about your marital status. Your options including: SINGLE, MARRIED/REMARRIED, SEPARATED, DIVORCED/WIDOWED. *(Hint: To my high school students, your boyfriend, girlfriend, or "BAE" classifies you as SINGLE)*

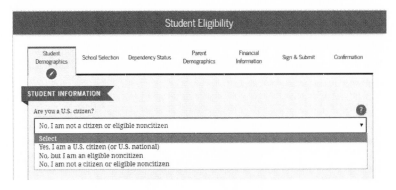

Student Demographics (Part VI)

In this section, you will be asked about your U.S. Citizenship. Your options including: Yes, I am a U.S. Citizen (U.S. national), No, but I am an eligible noncitizen, or No, I am not a citizen or eligible noncitizen.

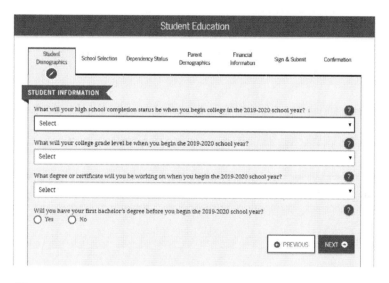

Student Demographics (Part VII)

In this section, you will be asked about your high school completion, college grade level, degree/cerification inquiries, and your degree status within the academic year.

Be prepared for the following subject matters and options to follow: **HIGH SCHOOL COMPLETION** (High school diploma, GED cerificate/state authorized high school equivalent certificate, Home schooled, None of the above); **COLLEGE GRADE LEVEL** (Never attended colelge/1st yr., Attended college before/1st yr., 2nd yr./sophomore, 3rd yr./junior, 4th yr/senior, 5th yr./other undergraduate, 1st yr. graduate professional, Continuing graduate/professional or beyond);

DEGREE/CERIFICATION INQUIRIES (1st bachelor's degree, 2nd bachelor's degree, Associate degree (occupational/technical program), Associate degree (general education/transfer program), Certificate/diploma (occupational/technical/education program of less than 2 yr.), Certificate/diploma (occupational/technical/education program of least more than 2 yr.), Teaching credential program (nondegree program), Graduate/professional degree,

Other/undecided); **DEGREE STATUS** (If you will have your first bachelors degree (four-year degree) before the academic year, click YES, if not, click NO.

Next, you will be asked about Federal Work-Study. Federal Work-Study offers part-time employment for undergraduate and graduate students with financial need. This allows students to earn money to assist in paying for education expenses. *I STRONGLY recommend you answering YES to this question.*

Follwing, you will be asked if you were a foster youth or were you ever in the foster care system. You will simply answer YES or NO. If your answer is YES, make sure to check with your school social worker, professional school counselor, and/or case worker for additonal information for college funding.

Finally, you will be asked about your parents (Parent 1 & Parent 2) about their highest school completed. Your options include: Middle School/Jr. High, High School, College or beyond, or Other/unknown.

FUN FACT #6:

Definitions of Higher Education Terms

Diploma: Offers a more in-depth curriculum; testifies that the recipient has successfully completed a course of study

Certification: Usual time length is two years or less of courses; certifications may include specific courses in a professional/technical field only

Associate Degree: Usually lasting two years or more; requires additional general education courses including: English, Mathematics, and Writing courses to round out the program; suited for students wanting to transfer to a four-year college

Bachelor's Degree: A degree that is earned by a student from a college or university usually after four years of study

Master's Degree: A degree that is earned by a student from a college or university usually after one to two years of study; this degree follows a bachelor's degree

Doctorate Degree: Highest academic degree; typically takes four or more years to complete

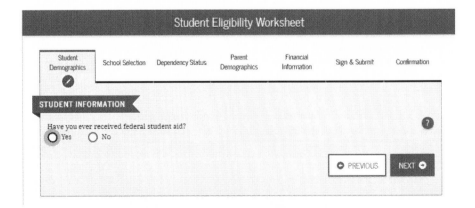

Student Demographics (Part VIII)

In this section, you will be asked if you received federal student aid before; this is a simple YES or NO. If answered YES, you will be asked if you have been convicted for the possession or sale of illegal drugs. If not, you will answer NO and if so, you will answer YES. In you were convicted, you will see this message: ***"If you are convicted of possessing or selling drugs after you submit your FAFSA, you must notify the financial aid administrator at your college immediately. You will lose your eligibility for federal student aid and will be required to pay back all aid you received after your conviction."***

School Selection (Part I)

In this section, you will be asked information about your high school. You will need to provide the following: **NAME OF HIGH SCHOOL, CITY OF HIGH SCHOOL**, and **STATE OF HIGH SCHOOL.** Once this information is entered, click the SEARCH button and you choose your correct high school.

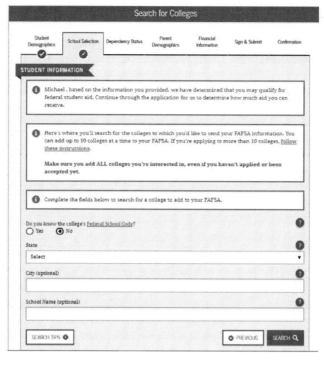

School Selection (Part II)

In this section, you will have the opportunity to choose ten (10) colleges you are interested in attending. They will receive your financial aid application once your application is submitted. There are two ways you can locate your colleges within the application database. 1) Each college has a FEDERAL SCHOOL CODE. If you know this code, enter it in the space provided. 2) If you do not know the code, enter the following information: **STATE, CITY (optional), SCHOOL NAME (optional).** Once this information is entered, your school of choice should be listed. With each college you enter, you will be asked about your housing plans; your options include: **ON CAMPUS, WITH PARENT, OFF CAMPUS**.

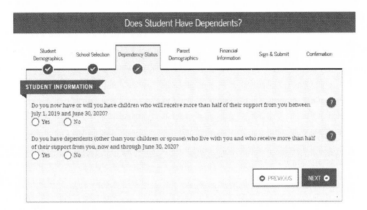

Dependency Status (Part I)

In this section, you (the student) will be asked about your dependents (if you have children). A dependent is a person who relies on another, especially a family member, for financial support. These questions are very straightforward; view the questions in the screenshot above. Once completed, press the NEXT button to continue with the application.

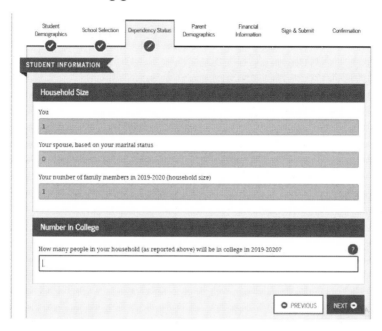

Dependency Status (Part II)

In this section, you will be answering questions about the size of your household. You will see questions like: **YOU** (the number "1" should already be populated, if not, enter it), **YOUR SPOUSE, BASED ON YOUR MARITAL STATUS** (this number should be populated from previous answers in your application; if not, enter it in the space provided), **HOUSEHOLD SIZE** (you will enter in this space the number of people who live in the same home as you), and **NUMBER IN COLLEGE** (you will enter in this space how many people in your home will be entering college during the academic year).

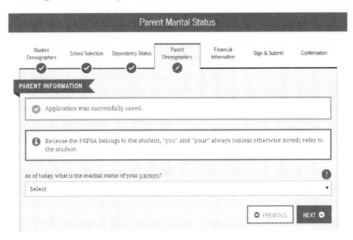

Parent Demographics

In this section, your parent(s) or legal guardian(s) will be providing information about themselves. This information will be ranged from marital status to tax information. Parents have to enter the following information:

Martial Status
Parent 1 and/or Parent 2: Social Security Number,
Last Name, First Name, & Date of Birth
Parents' Email-Address
Residency spanning five (5) years
Household Size
Household members in college

Parent Tax Information

This is where your parent(s) or legal guardian(s) will need their tax information to complete this part of the financial aid application. Be prepared for the following sections/questions:

Have parents completed their tax return?
-Already completed
-Will file
-Not going to file
Parents' filing status
-Single
-Head of Household
-Married-Filed Joint Return
-Married-Filed Separate Return
-Qualifying Widow(er)
-Don't Know

At this point, you are able to use the Data Retrieval
Tool by answering "NO" to the following:
-Did you, the parents, file an amended tax return?
-Did you, the parents, file a Puerto Rico or foreign tax
return?
-Did you, the parents, file taxes electronically in the
last 3 weeks (or mail in the last 11 weeks)?

**If not using the Data Retrieval Tool, continue with
application and answer the questions*

Type of income tax return filed
-IRS 1040
-IRS 1040A or 1040EZ
-Foreign tax return
-A tax return with Puerto Rico, a U.S. territory or
Freely Associated State

How much did Parent 1 earn from working?
(Enter an amount)

How much did Parent 2 earn from working?
(Enter an amount)

As of today, is either of your parents a dislocated worker?

Amount of parents' income tax

Parents' exemptions

Additional Financial Information/Untaxed Income

Parents' Current Assets

FUN FACT #7:

This graph displays information as to which tax information is needed for what academic year:

Tax Information Year	Academic Year
2018	2020-2021
2019	2021-2022
2020	2022-2023
2021	2023-2024
2022	2024-2025

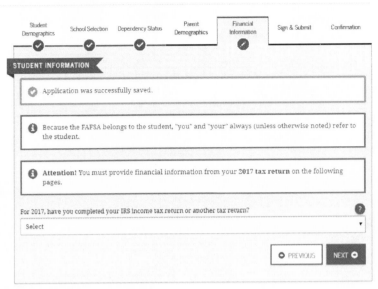

Student Tax Information

This is where you, the student, will need your tax information to complete this part of the financial aid application. Be prepared for the following sections/questions:

Have you completed their tax return?
-Already completed
-Will file
-Not going to file

At this point, you are able to use the Data Retrieval Tool by answering "NO" to the following:
-Did you, the parents, file an amended tax return?

-Did you, the parents, file a Puerto Rico or foreign tax return?

-Did you, the parents, file taxes electronically in the last 3 weeks (or mail in the last 11 weeks)?

If not using the Data Retrieval Tool, continue with application and answer the questions

Type of income tax return filed
-IRS 1040
-IRS 1040A or 1040EZ
-Foreign tax return
-A tax return with Puerto Rico, a U.S. territory or Freely Associated State

How much did you earn from working? (Enter an amount)

As of today, are you a dislocated worker?

Amount of your income tax

Your exemptions

Additional Financial Information/Untaxed Income

Current Assets

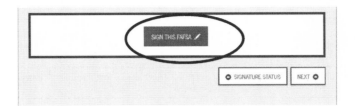

*The **IRS Data Retrieval Tool** allows applicants who have already filed their federal income tax returns to prefill the answers to some questions on the Free Application for Federal Student Aid (FAFSA) by transferring data from their federal income tax returns. This can save the family some time in completing the FAFSA.*

Sign & Submit

Guess what??!! This is the final stage of your financial aid application. Within this stage, you will be able to review your application. This is to make sure all information is accurate and completed. Once reviewed, you, the student, and your parent or guardian will sign the FAFSA using the FSA ID you applied for previously. Once you sign the FAFSA....you are DONE!!

Your confirmation page will be displayed. This page will show your estimated amount for the Pell Grant, Loans, and your EFC. What is EFC? Glad you asked! EFC stands for Expected Family Contribution. This concept tells you what funding (money) you can pay towards your education. If your EFC reads "0000," you are in a great place because you are more than likely to receive more funding.

Congratulations! You did it!

The FAFSA Mobile App
There's an app for that! You can now download the application for the FAFSA via your cellular phone and complete your application right at your fingertips!

Fun Fact #8:

Follow up with the institutions of your choosing to make sure your FAFSA has been received. Also, please check with for priority deadlines with your institutions for financial aid. THIS IS IMPORTANT!

The Finkley Experience. Section FIVE:
People Actually Give Me Money for College?

Crazy right? Total strangers giving you money for college; but it's true! This is why it is so important for you to do well in your academics, get involved within your community, join organizations, and complete your FAFSA. There are three ways in getting money for college; this is through: **GRANTS, SCHOLARSHIPS, and LOANS.** Hold on to your seats because I feel like I am about to blow your mind!

GRANTS

Grants are classified as "gifted aid." This is money given towards your cost of attendance for college. This is FREE money for you! When you see the terms "free money," you (the student) do not have to pay this money back. Aim for GRANTS!

Federal Pell Grants

The Federal Pell Grant is the most well-known of all

federal grants. To qualify for a Federal Pell Grant, you must show a financial need, be a US citizen, and be enrolled as an undergraduate student working towards your first undergraduate degree in an eligible program.

Federal Supplemental Education Opportunity Grants

The Federal Supplemental Education Opportunity Grants or FSEOG are for students that display a greater financial need based off a very low expected family contribution; students who qualify are also eligible for the Federal Pell Grant if they qualify.

FEDERAL WORK-STUDY PROGRAM

THIS IS NOT A GRANT! The Federal Work-Study Program offers funding for part time employment for eligible students. Not all institutions are eligible for this funding, so call your Office of Financial Aid to confirm. If you qualify for this program, you can use these funds

towards your cost of attendance or other expenses.
Remember, not all students will be eligible for this
program if you do not show a high financial need.

SCHOLARSHIPS

As the Founder, Melinda Mihlbauer, of P.A.C.E.
Scholarship Academy states often, "Full rides are
POSSIBLE!" Scholarships are also classified as "free
aid" is gift aid. This is money you DO NOT have to pay
back. Exciting, right? So, aim for SCHOLARSHIPS as
well! There are many national scholarships in the world.
Just think about your favorite shopping mall, the car you
drive, the clothes on your back, and the shoes on your
feet. What are you saying Finkley? Well, I am saying
nine times out of ten, they offer some type of scholarship.
Don't believe me? Do your own research and let me
know your findings!

If you are a graduating senior at your high school, your
professional school counselor, your career specialist, your

college counselor/coaches, and/or your high school scholarship coordinators should be your very best friend! These are the gatekeepers to free money. *I strongly recommend you visiting their offices at least once or twice a week.* They have the information to national scholarships and also local scholarships within your communities as well. Do not waste time, get on this task NOW! Free money also happens to go very fast!

Many of the institutions you are applying to offer scholarships for first-time freshman or for the two years or four years you may attend their institution. When applying to institutions, ask the Office of Admissions or Office of Financial Aid about need-based aid, merit-aid, institutional aid, and/or endowed scholarships. These are all monies coming from the institution to award students including what the federal government may award and other scholarships you may be appying for from your high school, community, etc.

FUN FACT #9:

Earlier I stated information about the P.A.C.E. Scholarship Academy. P.A.C.E. states for Professional Assistance states College-Prep Excellence. P.A.C.E. has prepared many students for college by assisting in the scholarship process by way of trainings and workshops. Melinda Mihlbauer has created a series of scholarship books for high school, undergraduate students, and graduate students. For more information, view her website at www.pacescholarshipacademy.com

LOANS

If grants and scholarships are not available to you, there are loans. Now, I would try to exhaust all other factors first, but at the end of the day, loans are here to assist. You must be careful in how you use these funds. PLEASE! PLEASE! DO NOT get monies if you do not need them. ***I STRONGLY recommend you getting the amount you need for your education and not worrying about getting a new car, clothes, etc. O yea...six***

months after graduation or if you fall below part time status, ranging 6-11 credit hours, you must begin the repayment process for loans. So again, choose wisely! Learn more about the federal loans offered:

Subsidized Stafford Loan

If your loan is subsidized, you will not be accountable for making any payments until after you graduate. The government pays your interest for you while you are attending your college/university. This type of loan is reserved for students who can show a financial hardship.

Unsubsidized Stafford Loan

If you have an unsubsidized loan, you are responsible for paying off all the interest. Typically, payments can be deferred or postponed until after graduation. All students are eligible for this type of loan.

Parent PLUS Loan

To be eligible for a Parent PLUS Loan, you (the student) must be enrolled at a qualifying institution and take at least a half-time course load. You and your parent/guardian must also meet the basic eligibility criteria. Contact your Office of Financial Aid to learn more about this criteria. Institutions of higher learning have different application processes for the Parent PLUS Loan; again, contact your Office of Financial Aid for more information.

PRIVATE EDUCATIONAL LOANS (NOT A FEDERAL LOAN)

With private loans, you can apply directly with the bank, financial institution, or lender that issues the loan. You can apply for private student loans when you need to; you must plan enough time for the lender to process your loan and distribute the monies requested to the institution of your choosing. If you are applying for a full year, your lender may disburse the funds to your institution each semester rather than all at once.

The Finkley Experience Section SIX:
Interviewing with College Officials

Picture it! You are on your first interview at the local fast food restaurant. You are nervous; you do not know what the employer is going to ask you and you are not sure what to ask the employer. Your heart is beating faster and faster until you sit down. You all begin to talk, and you think to yourself, "This is not too bad!" All your questions have come back to mind, you have gotten comfortable, and your confidence has gone through the roof; your true, authentic self has come onto the surface. This is the same concept when meeting with institutional officials in pursuing to gain admissions into a college/university.

First, find out whether interviews are required or optional. If the institution requires or offers interviews, contact the institution's Office of Admissions to find out what you must do to set one up. *I would highly recommend scheduling a campus tour for the same trip.*

The college interview, at times, is the deciding factor in being accepted, denied, or waitlisted you. This is an awesome time for admission counselors to get a chance to meet you face to face. The college interview gives you an opportunity to:

- ✓ Share information about yourself that was not included in your college application or your transcript
- ✓ Show your interest in the institution
- ✓ Discuss any issues with grades or behavior; be 100% honest and transparent
- ✓ Have an open conversation about your goals and dreams
- ✓ Ask as many questions about the institution as you can

You cannot pass or fail an interview, but please make a good impression by doing the following:

- ✓ Dress casually; this is not including jeans and a t-shirt

✓ Arrive early
✓ Be polite
✓ Avoid using slang or other inappropriate language
✓ Be confident but not arrogant
✓ Answer questions honestly

During the time, you will talk one-on-one with an admission counselor. If your parent/guardian comes with you, they may/may not be a part of the interview process. Remember, this process is all about the student! Again, the admission counselor wants to know about the student and why they should be admitted into their institution. Admission Counselor may ask the following questions:

✓ Tell me about yourself.
✓ Why did you choose our institution?
✓ What are your educational/career goals?
✓ How did you become interested in your major?
✓ What influenced your choice?
✓ What obstacles did you encounter while you were in high school?
✓ What are some of your proudest moments from high school?
✓ What are your favorite extracurricular activities?

✓ How are you going to contribute your skills and knowledge to our institution?

The admission counselor will also ask if you have any questions. Asking questions shows the admission counselor that you are interested in the institution, and it allows you to get information you cannot find via their website. After the interview, follow up with a thank you letter, email, and/or phone call.

The Finkley Experience. Section SEVEN: <u>*Playing Sports is NOT an Academic Major!*</u> <u>*It's a PLUS!*</u>

As an admission counselor/recruiter in my various positions, I have always asked the question, *"What do you want to major in?"* OR *"Where do you see you see yourself in the future?"* It never fails, when I hear, *"I want to major in basketball, soccer, or football."* At that moment, I am the barrier of bad news and tell them the hard truth…athletic programs are *NOT* academic programs! (Trust me, I do not scream at them.) But, in preparing to play sports for a college/university, there are some factors and qualifications that must come into play and they mainly start in the classroom.

One of the governing bodies for students wanting to pursue any athletic program in higher education is the **National Collegiate Athletic Association (NCAA).** The NCCA is a member-led organization devoted to the welfare and success of college athletes. This association

contains three divisions including: Division I, II, and III.
View the information below for requirements of the three
divisions:

Division I **(Full Qualifier)**	✓ Graduate high school ✓ Earn a core course GPA of 2.3 or higher ✓ Earn the ACT/SAT score matching your core-course GPA on the Division I sliding scale **Complete 16 core courses** 4 years of English 3 years of math (Algebra 1 or higher) 2 years of natural/physical science *(Including one year of lab, if offered)* 1 additional year of English, math or natural/physical science 2 years of social science 4 additional years of English, math, natural/physical science, social science, foreign language, comparative religion or philosophy ***You must complete 10 of the core courses by the end of your junior year (before the start of your seventh semester). Seven of the 10 core courses need to be in English, math or natural/physical science. The grades in these seven courses will be "locked in," meaning you will not be allowed to retake them to improve your grades.* ****College-bound student-athletes may practice, compete and receive athletics scholarships during their first year of enrollment at an NCAA Division I school.*

**This information is provided by www.ncaa.org*

Division I (Academic Redshirt)	✓ Graduate high school ✓ Earn a core course GPA of 2.0 or higher ✓ Earn the ACT/SAT score matching your core-course GPA on the Division I sliding scale **Complete 16 core courses** 4 years of English 3 years of math (Algebra 1 or higher) 2 years of natural/physical science *(Including one year of lab, if offered)* 1 additional year of English, math or natural/physical science 2 years of social science 4 additional years of English, math, natural/physical science, social science, foreign language, comparative religion or philosophy **You must complete 10 of the core courses by the end of your junior year (before the start of your seventh semester). Seven of the 10 core courses need to be in English, math or natural/physical science. The grades in these seven courses will be "locked in," meaning you will not be allowed to retake them to improve your grades.* ***College-bound student-athletes may receive athletics scholarships during their first year of enrollment and may practice during their first regular academic term, but may NOT compete during their first year of enrollment.*

DIVISION I FULL QUALIFIER SLIDING SCALE				DIVISION I FULL QUALIFIER SLIDING SCALE			
Core GPA	New SAT*	Old SAT (Prior to 3/2016)	ACT Sum	Core GPA	New SAT*	Old SAT (Prior to 3/2016)	ACT Sum
3.550	400	400	37	2.750	810	720	59
3.525	410	410	38	2.725	820	730	60
3.500	430	420	39	2.700	830	740	61
3.475	440	430	40	2.675	840	750	61
3.450	460	440	41	2.650	850	760	62
3.425	470	450	41	2.625	860	770	63
3.400	490	460	42	2.600	860	780	64
3.375	500	470	42	2.575	870	790	65
3.350	520	480	43	2.550	880	800	66
3.325	530	490	44	2.525	890	810	67
3.300	550	500	44	2.500	900	820	68
3.275	560	510	45	2.475	910	830	69
3.250	580	520	46	2.450	920	840	70
3.225	590	530	46	2.425	930	850	70
3.200	600	540	47	2.400	940	860	71
3.175	620	550	47	2.375	950	870	72
3.150	630	560	48	2.350	960	880	73
3.125	650	570	49	2.325	970	890	74
3.100	660	580	49	2.300	980	900	75
3.075	680	590	50	2.299	990	910	76
3.050	690	600	50	2.275	990	910	76
3.025	710	610	51	2.250	1000	920	77
3.000	720	620	52	2.225	1010	930	78
2.975	730	630	52	2.200	1020	940	79
2.950	740	640	53	2.175	1030	950	80
2.925	750	650	53	2.150	1040	960	81
2.900	750	660	54	2.125	1050	970	82
2.875	760	670	55	2.100	1060	980	83
2.850	770	680	56	2.075	1070	990	84
2.825	780	690	56	2.050	1080	1000	85
2.800	790	700	57	2.025	1090	1010	86
2.775	800	710	58	2.000	1100	1020	86

ACADEMIC REDSHIRT

**This information is provided by www.ncaa.org*

Division II (Full Qualifier)	✓ Graduate high school ✓ Earn a core course GPA of 2.20 or higher ✓ Earn the ACT/SAT score matching your core-course GPA on the Division II sliding scale **Complete 16 core courses** 3 years of English 2 years of math (Algebra 1 or higher) 2 years of natural/physical science *(Including one year of lab, if offered)* 3 additional year of English, math or natural/physical science 2 years of social science 4 additional years of English, math, natural/physical science, social science, foreign language, comparative religion or philosophy ****College-bound student-athletes may practice, compete and receive athletics scholarships during their first year of enrollment at an NCAA Division II school.*

**This information is provided by www.ncaa.org

Division II (Partial Qualifier)	✓ Graduate high school ✓ Earn a core course GPA of 2.00 or higher ✓ Earn the ACT/SAT score matching your core-course GPA on the Division II sliding scale **Complete 16 core courses** 3 years of English 2 years of math (Algebra 1 or higher) 2 years of natural/physical science *(Including one year of lab, if offered)* 3 additional year of English, math or natural/physical science 2 years of social science 4 additional years of English, math, natural/physical science, social science, foreign language, comparative religion or philosophy **** College-bound student-athletes may receive athletics scholarships during their first year of enrollment and may practice during their first regular academic term, but may NOT compete during their first year of enrollment.*

**This information is provided by www.ncaa.org

DIVISION II FULL QUALIFIER SLIDING SCALE					DIVISION II PARTIAL QUALIFIER SLIDING SCALE			
USE FOR DIVISION II BEGINNING AUGUST 2018					USE FOR DIVISION II BEGINNING AUGUST 2018			
Core GPA	New SAT*	Old SAT (Prior to 3/2016)	ACT Sum		Core GPA	New SAT*	Old SAT (Prior to 3/2016)	ACT Sum
3.300 & above	400	400	37		3.050 & above	400	400	37
3.275	410	410	38		3.025	410	410	38
3.250	430	420	39		3.000	430	420	39
3.225	440	430	40		2.975	440	430	40
3.200	460	440	41		2.950	460	440	41
3.175	470	450	41		2.925	470	450	41
3.150	490	460	42		2.900	490	460	42
3.125	500	470	42		2.875	500	470	42
3.100	520	480	43		2.850	520	480	43
3.075	530	490	44		2.825	530	490	44
3.050	550	500	44		2.800	550	500	44
3.025	560	510	45		2.775	560	510	45
3.000	580	520	46		2.750	580	520	46
2.975	590	530	46		2.725	590	530	46
2.950	600	540	47		2.700	600	540	47
2.925	620	550	47		2.675	620	550	47
2.900	630	560	48		2.650	630	560	48
2.875	650	570	49		2.625	650	570	49
2.850	660	580	49		2.600	660	580	49
2.825	680	590	50		2.575	680	590	50
2.800	690	600	50		2.550	690	600	50
2.775	710	610	51		2.525	710	610	51
2.750	720	620	52		2.500	720	620	52
2.725	730	630	52		2.475	730	630	52
2.700	740	640	53		2.450	740	640	53
2.675	750	650	53		2.425	750	650	53
2.650	750	660	54		2.400	750	660	54
2.625	760	670	55		2.375	760	670	55
2.600	770	680	56		2.350	770	680	56
2.575	780	690	56		2.325	780	690	56
2.550	790	700	57		2.300	790	700	57
2.525	800	710	58		2.275	800	710	58
2.500	810	720	59		2.250	810	720	59
2.475	820	730	60		2.225	820	730	60
2.450	830	740	61		2.200	830	740	61
2.425	840	750	61		2.175	840	750	61
2.400	850	760	62		2.150	850	760	62
2.375	860	770	63		2.125	860	770	63
2.350	860	780	64		2.100	860	780	64
2.325	870	790	65		2.075	870	790	65
2.300	880	800	66		2.050	880	800	66
2.275	890	810	67		2.025	890	810	67
2.250	900	820	68		2.000	900	820 & above	68 & above
2.225	910	830	69					
2.200	920	840 & above	70 & above					

*Final concordance research between the new SAT and ACT is ongoing.

This information is provided by www.ncaa.org

FACT # 10:

Understanding your NCAA Academic Status

Final Qualifier: You meet all of the academic requirements and can receive an athletic scholarship your first year.	**Early Academic Qualifier**: This status is based on your academic record after six semesters of high school. It means you are eligible to receive an athletic scholarship and practice/compete with your team during your first year of full-time college enrollment. Make sure to meet with your college's compliance office to confirm this status.	**Final Nonqualifier**: You do not meet the academic requirements and are not eligible to compete or practice at the college requesting your final status. You will not be eligible to receive an athletic scholarship.	**Final Partial Qualifier**: This is a status for only DII schools. Athletes with this status can receive an athletic scholarship and practice with the team, but you are not eligible to compete your first year in college.	**Under Review**: The NCAA Eligibility Center is reviewing a unique academic situation related to your case.
Academic Redshirt: This means you will be eligible to receive an athletic scholarship and practice but will not be allowed to compete during your first year in school. Only athletes enrolling in a Division I school after August 1, 2016, are eligible for this status.	**Automatic Waiver Approved**: This indicates that you are immediately eligible to receive an athletic scholarship, and practice/compete with your team during your first year as a full-time enrollee. Contact your college's compliance department for more details.	**HS Decision Pending**: If your high school courses are not NCAA Approved, the NCAA will likely need to make a more in-depth review of your high school classes.	**In Process**: The NCAA Eligibility Center is reviewing your case. Usually, cases remain in process for no more than two business days.	**Secondary Review**: On rare occasions, the NCAA will make a secondary review of your status. This will only happen with the help your college compliance office.

Waiver Approved: From time to time, your colleges compliance office will file for a waiver if they think you will meet one of the cases for academic waivers. This status means that waiver has been approved.	Waiver Denied: If your compliance office has filed for a waiver and it is denied, you will receive this status. This likely means you will not be eligible for a scholarship or to compete.	Waiver Partially Approved (athletics aid only): If your compliance office has filed for a waiver on your behalf, it might be partially approved. This would mean you are eligible to receive an athletic scholarship but are not eligible to practice or play your first year in college.	Waiver Partially Approved (aid and practice): If your compliance office has filed for a waiver on your behalf, this status would mean you are eligible to receive an athletic scholarship and practice, but you will not be eligible to compete your first year in college.	COLLEGE SPORTS

**This information is provided by* www.ncsasports.org

If you are considering another avenue of playing sports while in college, think about the **National Association of Intercollegiate Athletics (NAIA)**. The NAIA is a college athletics association for small colleges and universities in North America. The NAIA includes two divisions (Division I and II). Division I in the NAIA is comparable to Division II in the NCAA. View the following eligibility requirements:

U.S. Freshman	Incoming U.S. freshmen need to fulfill and provide documentation for two of the following three criteria: ✓ Athletes who take their standardized tests between March 1, 2016 and May 1, 2019 need to achieve a minimum of a 16 on the ACT or 860 on the SAT. After May 1, 2019, athletes must get either an 18 on the ACT or a 970 on the SAT. Athletes must have the testing centers send their scores directly to the NAIA using the code **9876**. ✓ Achieve a minimum overall high school grade point average of 2.0 on a 4.0 scale. Athletes need to send their official transcript to the NAIA, either via the High School Portal or as a hard copy in the mail. ✓ Graduate in the top half of their high school class. If this information isn't included on the athlete's official transcript, the athlete needs to provide a class rank letter. ****The academic requirements for GED students are the same as incoming freshmen, except they cannot use class rank. They must meet both the GPA and test score requirements instead, and the successful completion of the GED immediately fulfills the GPA requirements. GED students should have their ACT or SAT scores sent to the*

	eligibility center directly from the testing service using the NAIA's code: 9876. They also need to have their official GED information sent to the eligibility center.

**This information is provided by www.ncsasports.org*

International Freshman	Students who finished high school outside of the U.S. or its territories must meet two of the following three requirements and provide the correct documentation: ✓ Achieve a minimum of 16 on the ACT or 860 on the SAT ✓ Achieve a minimum overall high school grade point average of 2.0 on a 4.0 scale ✓ Graduate in the top half of their high school class

**This information is provided by www.ncsasports.org*

Transfer Students	Transfer students from both two-year and four-year universities who have never played on an NAIA team must register with the NAIA Eligibility Center. To be eligible, they must: ✓ Have a minimum of a 2.0 GPA from all previous colleges combined. The athlete will need to have all official transcripts from each college or university they have attended sent to the NAIA. ✓ Meet all conference-specific requirements for transfers. This will vary from conference to conference and the athlete should

	check their To Do List in their profile to determine the additional steps they should take. ✓ Provide proof of graduation from high school. The athlete can have an official high school transcript sent to the NAIA via the High School Portal or they can send a hard copy in the mail. ✓ Provide a list of all their competitive experiences—both collegiate and non-collegiate—since high school graduation. Athletes simply need to add this list in their online NAIA Profile.

**This information is provided by www.ncsasports.org*

Homeschooled Students	Home schooled students only need to meet the test score requirements and provide the NAIA with their home school transcript. The transcript must include a graduation date and a signature by the home school administrator. Students who take their standardized tests between March 1, 2016 and May 1, 2019 need to get a score of an 18 ACT or a 950 SAT. If they do not meet the test score requirement, they can request a home school waiver from the NAIA Home School Committee.

**This information is provided by www.ncsasports.org*

Now, let's look at the **National Junior College Athletic Association (NJCAA)**. The NJCAA governs community college, state college and junior college athletics throughout the United States. Per the NJCAA for initial eligibility, the association states, "Due to the unique academic and athletic situation of each individual, and the complexity of the NJCAA eligibility rules, it is recommended that each potential student-athlete discuss their athletic eligibility with the athletic personnel at the NJCAA college where they have chosen to attend. Should the athletic staff have any questions in determining an individual's eligibility, the college may contact the NJCAA National Office for assistance." For more in-depth information about eligibility, visit the NJCAA Website at www.njcaa.org.

Let's discuss the **National Christian College Athletic Association (NCCAA)**. The National Christian College Athletic Association is an association of Christian universities, colleges, and Bible colleges in the United States and Canada. The NCCAA consist of two divisions; these includes Divisions I and Division II.

View the following eligibility requirements:

Division I Entering First-Year Students	An entering freshman student must meet two of the three entry level requirements: ✓ A score of 18 or higher on the Enhanced ACT OR a score of 860 or higher on the SAT. ✓ A minimum overall high school grade point average of 2.00 on a 4.00 scale. ✓ Graduation in the upper half of the student's high school graduating class.

**This information is provided by www.thenccaa.org*

Division I G.E.D. Students	(General Education Diploma) Students: ✓ GED students must achieve a minimum of 18 on the Enhanced ACT or 860 on the SAT. ✓ GED students are recognized as having met the GPA requirement. ✓ Class rank requirement is not applicable in regard to GED.

**This information is provided by www.thenccaa.org*

	HOME Schooled Students: ✓ Must achieve a minimum of 18 on the Enhanced ACT or 860 on the SAT ✓ Must receive the certificate (or equivalent) granted by the

Division I HOME Schooled Students	appropriate state verifying successful completion of home schooling requirements. If the state does not issue certificates (or equivalent) the case must go to the NCCAA National Eligibility Committee. ✓ Class rank requirement is not applicable. *** (NOTE: Home school students who have a 20 on the Enhanced ACT or 950 on the SAT are considered to have met the freshman eligibility requirement.)*

***This information is provided by www.thenccaa.org*

Division I International Students	International Students: The same three criteria listed above are to be used. However, if the foreign high school transcript is such that the grade point average cannot be determined and the class ranking is not available, the foreign student can be ruled eligible by meeting the specific institution's admission criteria for foreign students and by meeting the following NCCAA criteria: ✓ A score of 18 or higher on the Enhanced ACT OR 860 or higher on the SAT. ✓ Meet the requirements listed in the most current Guide to International Academic Standards for Athletics Eligibility (GIAS) published by the NCAA (based on AACRAO guidelines).

***This information is provided by www.thenccaa.org*

Division II	For more information, contact the Office of Athletics at the institution(s) of your interest.

** *This information is provided by* <u>www.thenccaa.org</u>

Finally, let's discuss the **United States Collegiate Athletic Association (USCAA)**. The USCAA is a national organization for the intercollegiate athletic programs that are mostly small colleges, community colleges and junior colleges, across the United States. View the following eligibility requirements:

24.5   Eligibility Requirements

For a student to be eligible for any intercollegiate competition, a member institution must ensure that the student conforms to the following regulations:

24.5.1 High School Graduate or GED

The student must be a graduate of an accredited high school or have earned a graduate equivalent degree (GED).

24.5.2 Academic Progress

All students must be enrolled in a recognized academic program and be making progress toward a 2/4 year degree at the attending college.

24.5.3 Full-time Enrollment

All students must be enrolled in a minimum of 12 credits at time of participation. If a student is enrolled in less than 12 credits, he/she will be considered part-time for eligibility purposes.

24.5.4 Requirements for Students Entering Second Semester

Second semester students must have achieved a GPA of 1.6.

24.5.5 Requirements after the First Two Semesters

All students must pass 24 credit hours the previous academic school year. If there is a break in attendance the student athlete must pass 24 credit hours the two preceding terms of attendance.

Exception
a. If a freshman completes his/her first semester at an institution and leaves the following semester, upon the student's return he/she may reestablish their eligibility by completing the necessary credits to reach 12 during a summer or interim period only. *(Revised 03/19/12)*

24.5.6 GPA Requirements after the First Two Semesters

After accumulating 24-48 credit hours, the student must have achieved a 1.75 cumulative GPA. After accumulating more than 48 credit hours, the student must have achieved a 2.0 GPA.

**This information is provided by www.uscaa.prestosport.com

The Finkley Experience Section EIGHT:
Is College Really for Me?

There is a major push for college in society today. Yes, this is a GREAT thing, but is college really the route for everyone? If you have a set goal in mind, do not allow anyone to take that away from you. I would advice you to conduct proper research. You would be surprised that your ulimiate goal may not even require a two-year or four-year degree. Take a look at the various alternatives:

Career Education Focused Institutions

Picture it! You are watching television and this commerical comes on and says you can become a medical assistant in just eight months. Does this ring a bell? Well, it should! Within these institutions, they specialize in a particular program areas; for example: healthcare (medical assisting, nursing assistant, massage therapy, pharamacy technician), welding, automatic technician, and the list continues. The purpose of these institutions are to provide a faster method for students to obtain a certification and start working within their field of choice in less than twelve months. When it comes to financing this type of education, it can be a costly; but if you do your research correctly and you know this is the route you would like to take, DO IT!

Military

A lot of my students I have mentored over the years have decided to go this route in joining the military. Within learning about themselves, they reaped the benefits of what the military has to offer. I am proud to say that my dad, brother, and step-father have all been a product of the US Armed Forces. I know many of you are thinking about doing the same as you are whining down your high school years. Right? Again, I encourage you to do your research and keep your grades up as well. You will need to take the Armed Services Vocational Aptitude Battery (ASVAB). The test measures competency in nine different subjects, which includes General Science, Electronics Information, Auto and Shop Information, Mechanical Comprehension, Assembling Objects, Word Knowledge, Paragraph Comprehension, Arithmetic Reasoning, and Mathematics Knowledge. These last four sections- Word Knowledge, Paragraph Comprehension, Arithmetic Reasoning, and Mathematics Knowledge are the most important, as they make up something called the AFQT (Armed Forces Qualifications Test). An applicant's AFQT score is what determines whether or not they are able to serve in the military at all, as each branch has minimum scores for enlistment (this information is provided by *www.uniontestprep.com*). Below are the scores for each of the branches in the United States:

Armed Force Branches	Score Requirements
Air Force	Minimum AFQT score of 36. Minimum score of 65 required if applicant has a high school equivalency degree (GED, TASC, HiSET) but has not completed at least 15 hours college credit.
Army	Minimum AFQT score of 31. Minimum score of 50 required for an applicant holding a high school equivalency degree (GED, TASC, HiSET).
Coast Guard	Minimum AFQT score of 40. Those holding a high school equivalency degree (GED, TASC, HiSET) need a score of at least 50 and should have at least 15 hours of college credit.
Marine Corps	Minimum AFQT score of 32. Minimum score of 50 required for an applicant holding a high school equivalency degree (GED, TASC, HiSET).
Navy	Minimum AFQT score of 35. Those holding a high school equivalency degree (GED, TASC, HiSET) need a score of at least 50 and should have at least 15 hours of college credit.

**This information comes from www.uniontestprep.com as of August 2019*

Service Learning

Do you like giving back to your community? Are you actively involved in clubs and organizations that benefit your high school, fellow classmates, and community? Well, have you ever thought about conintuing these efforts once you graduate high school? You can! View the opportunities that are avaliable to you:

AmeriCorps offers a variety of service opportunities, from the classroom to the outdoors, and everything in between. No matter what you are passionate about, where you are from, or why you choose to serve, AmeriCorps is your chance to be the greater good. Different AmeriCorps programs have different qualifications. In general, you will need to be at least 17 or 18 years old and a U.S. citizen or national or lawful permanent resident.

Visit their website @ https://www.nationalservice.gov/programs/americorps

City Year helps to close gaps in high-need schools by supporting students' academic and social-emotional development while also providing schools with the additional capacity to enhance school culture and climate. You must be able to dedicate 11 months to full-time service. Be between the ages of 18 and 25. Be a U.S. citizen or legal permanent resident alien. Have served no more than 3 terms in another AmeriCorps, NCCC or VISTA program.

Visit their website @ www.cityyear.org

Mission trips and other faith-forming experiences are proven to be the #1 way to keep teens active in the church and growing in their faith. SERVE youth mission trips for teens are all-inclusive, 5-7 day service trips for Middle School or High School students. The students go into communities in the USA and Canada to care for and restore their world in an environment where they'll encounter the concepts of justice and missional living. More than just a week-long short-term mission trip over the summer, SERVE is a

faith-forming experience where the communities, congregations, and students who are involved all experience lasting transformation.

Visit their website @ www.youthunlimited.org

Professional Employment

When I was in high school, I had a part time job at a local fast-food restaurant. When I was thinking about dropping out of college, I had a PLAN B in motion. I contacted my former manager and told her I was dropping out and I wanted to be trained as a manager. She was so excited that she completed the paperwork right away. When I decided to stay in college, I was relieved that I could always have an alternative. As you see in my example, instead of asking for my former position of crew member, I asked to be a manager. Now, if you plan to go in the workforce after graduating high school, be smart, effective, and productive about this choice. You always want to go forward in life and never backwards. Follow

these tips when it comes to employment after high
school:

- If you already have a job while in high school, learn
  all you can about the industry (i.e. restaurant,
  hospitialty, retail); your knowledge will make you
  marketable.

- Always have a mindset of moving upward in a
  company.

- If you do not have a job while you are in high school
  and you maybe are looking for employment, allow
  yourself to be trainable by having an open mind.

- When submitting applications and going on
  interviews, you will be asked for the following
  documents: cover letter, résumé, and professional
  references. For these documents, refer to *The
  Finkley Experience Workbook* under the *Career
  Readiness section* for guidance.

- Always have a mind set of "How can I contribute to this company?" "How can I improve this company?"

- Always practice your interview questions and your communication skills.

- Always dress the part; meaning know what to wear and NOT to wear during the interview process.

- When chatting with the interviewer, learn their name and repeat their name (not repeatedly, but sporadically) throughout the interview.

- Always smile, be positive, and be confident!

The Finkley Experience Section NINE:
Finkley's Advice to You!

Well, you are here! I have shared my experiences, knowledge, and wisdom with you I have learned throughout my time in the profession of secondary and higher education. Just know this, I am PROUD of you! You have decided to take a part of an educational jounrey many are afraid to take on. This shows me you are determined and dedicated to yourself. Please, never loose this quality. I am talking from experience; you will go far in life. Now that you have this entire college process down like a pro, let me give you some advice as to what to do when you arrive to college. You ready? Let's go!

I.   **CHOOSING A ROOMMATE**- At most institutions, you have the ability to choose your roommate. If you do not have a roommate in mind; no worries! You will take a compatibility assessment. Within this assessment, the institution will discovery what your likes are as a student; they will then match you with another student similar to your background. Cool, right? You will normally know who your rommate is before you move into your dormitory. Make sure you contact your roommate. Please get to know them as a person first. Please become familiar with the policies and procedures of your dormitory. Always remember if you have any problems with each other, contact your residential assistant/director. DO NOT try to handle it yourself!

II. **CHOOSING A MEAL PLAN**- I am talking from experience here; college food is the BEST food, to me! When I arrived on the campus of Allen University, Columbia, SC, I did not know once you finished your plate of food, you can go back and get as many as you want. It was so much fun! When choosing a meal plan at an institution, it can be challenging sometimes. Many institutions have many to choose from while other institutions have only one plan for everyone to follow. DO YOUR RESEARCH! Remember, your meal plan is covered in your cost of attendance. It is listed as "ROOM and BOARD." This means your lodging and food. Again, choose wisely; if you eat a lot, get the biggest meal plan you can afford; if you do not eat a lot, get the smaller meal plan. This difference assists with how much you are paying to attend yearly.

III. **FRESHMAN FIFTEEN (POUNDS)**- When it comes to your health, you have to monitor it. If you are not daily doing some sort of exercise, you will easily gain weight. I went to college in a metro-city. My friends and I, would walk everywhere just for fun. This was fun and exciting because we were experiencing this together. I was able to maintain my weight and not gain any weight. You always have to remember to take care of youself FIRST!

IV. **HEALTH INSURANCE**- Do you have this? Most institutions of higher learning instruct their students to have health insurance. But, if students are under the age of 26, they can be covered by their parent's health care plan; this is in part to the Patient Protection and Affordable Care Act (PPACA). By being covered under your parent's plan, you (as the student) have the opportunity to waive the health insurance plan offered by your institution. DO YOUR RESEARCH!

V. **SECURITY**- By law, each college/university must provide a report of incidents that have taken place on their campus. This data collection is required by the Jeanne Clery Disclosure of Campus Security Policy, the Campus Crime Statistics Act, and the Higher Education Opportunity Act. It must be placed on the institution's website yearly. Please familiarize yourself with your campus security. If you do not feel safe at any time, please inform them immediately. Always ask questions about your safety.

VI.   **ACADEMICS/ASK FOR HELP**- The reason you are paying to attend an university/college is to obtain a degree or certification; right? In this process of learning, you are going to run into many subjects within your program of study you have no clue of what the professor is talking about. Well, ask for help! This is why professors, instructors, and tutors are there; to assist you! They want you to excel, they want you to do your personal best, they want you to graduate. Take advantage of the help they are providing for you. Again, your goal is to graduate!

VII. **SOCIALIZING**- I truly believe college is supposed to be a setting where you learn, but also to have FUN as well (not too much). The reason I was about to drop out of college was not because of academics (I was doing very well), but I was not active on my campus. I later joined clubs, organizations, I was initiated into a fraternity, and joined the choir. The more I became active, the more I fell in love with my institution and did not want to leave. I challenge you to become active on your new community.

VIII. **MEET NEW, LIKE-MINDED PEOPLE**- The best part about college is discoverying who you are as an individual. With that discovery, your goal is to determine the people in your life; do they lift me up? Or do they tear me down? If they lift you up and you lift them up, they are a keeper. If they show no support, if they discourage you everytime you have a goal you want to obtain, or if they have no growth mindset, let them go! My friends in my circle I have now are AWESOME! We dream together, support one another, and pray together. When I chat with any of them, I get a positive charge to do better with my life. If I do better within my own life, I am able to be that much more effective to the people I come across on a daily basis. Remember, your circle of friends is a reflection of you!

IX.   **ADDITIONAL SERVICES-** When I was a College and Career Counselor, I had the pleasure of serving 9th-12th graders. This was so rewarding. From this, I was able to learn more about students with learning accomodations. Having learning accomodations is not a terrible thing at all, it is just another resource for students. But, did you know that some of those same accomodations can follow you into college? Cool, right? I would definitely reach out to your institution's Office of Admissions for more information. Do not be ashamed; remember what I said previously…ASK FOR HELP!

X.   **NETWORKING-** Meeting people is great! So, how are you going to make these connections work for you? First, create a business card; nothing too much. On your cards, include your NAME, EMAIL, and PHONE NUMBER. If your social media is appropriate, include your various handles as well. If your social media is NOT appropriate, FIX IT! With the people you are meeting, keep in contact with them bi-monthly; nothing too annoying, but well enough for them to remember your name. As you continue through your college years, attend as many professional functions as you possibly can. You never know who will be there. Also, please act accordingly. You never know who is watching you.

XI. **AFTER COLLEGE-** It is great to meet awesome people and graduate with a degree/certification, but what are you going to do with it? During your sophomore year (usually this the time a student takes taking classes in their major at a four-year institituion), start developing a plan for your professional life after graduating. If you need assistance, please reach out to your academic advisor or visit your Career Center at your institution. These people are trained to assist you with your career readiness needs. This is a great tool to assist you in finding what you really want to do within the program you are studying. Start asking yourself questions: *"Do I want to obtain a graduate degree?" "Does my program require me to be certified?" "Can I recieve employment with the degree/certification I will be obtaining?"* Once a plan is in place, follow it. Now, life does happen and

things will change; just modify and adjust and keep
pushing towards graduation. You got this!

Again, I am soooo proud of you! You are doing it and, I
know, you will do it well. You are getting the same
advice about college readiness as if you were to come
into my office to have a face-to-face conversation. I am
excited for you and this awesome journey. Remember,
you were already made GREAT, now strive for
GREATNESS!

Be blessed!

Made in the USA
Columbia, SC
06 August 2020